Gravity

Gravity

New & Selected Poems

by Donna Hilbert

MOON TIDE PRESS

2025

Editor-in-chief
Eric Morago

Associate Editor
Mackensi E. Green

Editor Emeritus
Michael Miller

Marketing/Social Media Specialist
Ellen Webre

Operations Associate
Shelly Holder

Cover art
Miriam Berkely

Author photo
Alexis Rhone Fancher

Book design
Michael Wada

Moon Tide logo design
Abraham Gomez

Gravity: New & Selected Poems (Second Edition)
is published by Moon Tide Press

Moon Tide Press
6709 Washington Ave. #9297
Whittier, CA 90608
www.moontidepress.com

SECOND EDITION

Printed in the United States of America

ISBN # 978-1-957799-30-8

For my beloved family,
for Nathaniel, for my workshop,
and for my family of friends.

Death is the mother of beauty, mystical,
Within whose burning bosom we devise
our earthly mothers waiting, sleeplessly.

from "Sunday Morning"
—Wallace Stevens

Contents

What to Believe: New Poems

Objects Brought from my Mother's House

Philosophy

Foreword

If you observe Donna Hilbert in a room or on the street meeting friends, you will bear witness to the ability of human beings to light up. It seems to happen simultaneously, in an all-at-once-ness. I would like to someday see a high-speed camera recording of it, played back in super-slow motion to discover where that spark initiates: In Donna's eyes and face, or the friend's? In Donna's hands reaching out, perhaps. It is a brightening that seems both spontaneous and instantaneous.

I feel the same when I read Donna's poetry, which is some of my favorite writing to be found anywhere. There is some immediate illumination that happens—between objects and observations in the poem, between the music of the language and the subject conveyed—and it comes from the page, yes, initiating literally from the author's eyes and hands reaching out. I feel brighter in these moments. Both physically and intellectually. Intimately. The way Nils Bohr said paired atoms are able to simultaneously reverse their spins as if one thing.

So this is all about some sort of connectedness. My high-falutin' metaphors here do not do it justice, and are more stilted than Donna's words will ever be—although I have always felt a kinship with her and a shared sensibility about the world, and I am reminded of this time and again from her writings, which point out our shared humanity and the bonds often overlooked. It may all seem like magic, but it's really just about paying attention. A way of respecting the common behavior of things found spinning in unison in our day-to-day world. And Donna Hilbert is brilliant at locating such precise gifts and offering them to us, as effortlessly and naturally as one might offer a slice of orange in an outstretched hand. George Saunders once said in an interview: "Empathy is a funny word because it's loaded with this kind of 'feel good' thing, but it revises *you* toward precision, which I think is a form of affection. If I really want to know you and I get all of your details, that's a kind of a form of love." Yes, so it's not just the intelligence of the storytelling here, but the empathy rendered via precision of detail—yet this complex craft all flows naturally, confident enough to not have to call attention to itself. Illumination of the commonplace and the grace of things in a language that is just right for the subject, and human, and humane. All without showing off. All in service of the poem. Which is in service of our shared gestures and conversations and embraces, in quiet rooms and on crowded streets—the resonances of our moments together, lit up anew by the artist. That's what you will find here in this collection. And even if you've never read her work or met Donna Hilbert before now, you will walk away feeling hugged, and brighter for it.

Grant Hier Anaheim, 2017

Gravity

What binds me to this earth
are the hands of my children,
as I hold my mother
holding her mother
back to the mother
who begat us all.
This is gravity.
This is why we call the earth
Mother, why all rising is a miracle.

From *Transforming Matter*

Redemption depends on the tiny fissure in the continuous catastrophe

—Walter Benjamin

Dove

Death mothered beauty
on the sliding glass door
where the ring-necked dove
flew toward the kitchen.
What's left on glass—
more brass rubbing
than fossil—
imprint in feathers and dust,
beak, head, wings
rising slightly in surprise.

Proof

Roses, my dog,
sleeps on her back,
paws raised to the sun,
as if a gift will appear
while she rests.
Tiny miracle of design
lavished underside her paws:
star of black hair
made to pat upon the ground.
Star bounding the four-pad crown
from the soft triangle of flesh.
I think of St. Thomas Aquinas—
the fifth proof for the existence of God—
I'm certain that I do believe
in Roses my dog.

August

August and the flies are slow,
ooze yellow pudding
when squashed
between my palms.
Ants sting my sleep,
crawl across my body
to the ant trap beneath the bed.
Daddy long-legs
rappel from every corner.
Standing on a foot stool,
I broom them down.
When we first moved in,
crickets ruled the house.
To not disturb our luck,
we trapped and placed
each one outdoors.
Soon chirping and jumping
became bad luck enough
and we paid the children
for every cricket killed.
It's easy now
to erase the snails
who eat our basil.
Listen how their shells click—
a wrinkling of paper—
smashing again
against the asphalt street.

Six Genre

Novel

Anna under the train,
Emma's apothecary poison,
and my late-twentieth century
life meanders, lacks plot.
Character and conflict
appear in abundance and on cue,
but I shrink from the climax,
not wanting the denouement
to occur without me.

Short Story

It's true. The end
and beginning are hard,
but in between is bliss—
the gold coin of revelation—
with no further chapter
in which the piper appears
demanding to be paid
for the unconsidered slap,
the awful kiss.

Poem

I throw my shoulder
out of socket hurtling
lightning from the dark,
portentous clouds.
It's not enough
to touch the gods,
I want to be one.
I think I am, in fact,
levitating here with you,
while below us
children cry
and want their supper.

Movie

In this re-make
the plot is hackneyed
but well-wrought
and the star turns reverse for twist:
she refuses to leave her husband
while he fears he's just an object used
for sex.
Distraught, she tumbles
from plot point to plot point
praying *deus exmachina*
save me. Save me.

Play

Better to rise and fall
in one act.

Problems with the second
are classic:
everyone on stage to explain—
no ecstasy, all exposition.

What is sadder than the curtain on act three?
Extra time, to be sure,
but we fall on the sword
just the same.

Opera

Every night while I cook dinner
Mimi dies
in grand voice, consumptive
under a blood-spumed Paris moon.

How can there be more suffering than this?

Every night to die for passion,
yet be forced alive
assigned the living task of chopping onion,
smashing buds of garlic with a spoon.

Poem to my First Love

Because our fathers
were too drunk
to pick us up
from the high school dance,
you walked me home
three miles
down dark empty
valley streets,
past tract houses
past orange groves
whose pungent blooms
perfumed the still night air.
I remember your black hair,
green eyes, the cleft
of your chin.
At fifteen, you were
six-foot-four
size fourteen shoe.
Your father beat you
and when he couldn't anymore
drop-kicked you
from the house, instead.
In school, you were famous
for being handsome, smart
for football, and lighting
cherry bombs
at lunch time on the quad.

You'd be a doctor, you said
on our slow-walk home
not a plumber
like your father
his life all shit
and tight spaces
no wonder he'd become
a drunk.

Sweat-suit

My father lies on the floor
by the open patio door
engaged in an afternoon
snooze. His chest rises
beneath his brown
sweat-suit, carried up
down, by the underground
force of his breath.
Geologic—the bellow, gurgle
of his body at rest.

In the last photograph
he wears that sweat-suit—
cotton thin at the elbows,
knees, showing pin-points
of skin. Thin, like the fabric
of his heart, stretching,
a cheap balloon,
every beat, a beat closer
to its final bursting.

City of Lakewood

I

City of Lakewood's
orange vested workers chop
jacarandas into stumps.
I see this as I exit the 605
 driving east on Del Amo.
The trees strike-slip
the sidewalk with their roots.
I guess this the excuse
to hack the jacarandas
to the ground.
What, come June, will console
us on the gray gloom days
without the trees'
profligate purple gown?
But now, it's February.
I turn north on Bloomfield,
enter Cerritos, a newer town,
with parkways of pear trees
in winter-white regalia
still years from bursting
concrete with their roots.

II
City of Lakewood
are you jealous of the tree
living in three worlds
at once?

City of Lakewood
do you fear the secret of the tree?
In the democracy of carbon
we are one.

III
City this is that doesn't love a tree.
City of Lakewood.
There is no lake here,
and soon, I fear, no wood.

From *Traveler in Paradise*

What cannot be said will bewept

—Sappho

Friday Nights

Friday nights, my father sat
in his green *Naugahyde* chair
smoking, drinking beer,
the red tip of his cigarette
tracing the pathway
from the ashtray to his lips.
My father sat in his chair
like a storm sits on the horizon,
gathering flash and clap
to slam across the prairie.
Friday nights, I flattened
thinner than a paper doll,
shrank smaller than a crayon,
knowing the tallest presence
takes the lightning.
If my father were a storm
building on the horizon,
if our house were on the prairie,
I could blow out the door,
down the concrete stairs
into the dark, damp cellar
to safety.

Angels

for Jill Young

Angels file their nails, floss their teeth,
play charades and trivial pursuit,
always taking pains to keep
their fingers busy
knowing full well to be idle—
even for angels—begs trouble.
Angels in raiment
of virginal lingerie
repose on chaise lounges
while watching the world
like mid-season TV—
re-runs of arguments, car chases,
armies amassing at borders.
Angels are helpless to act
until someone asks.
Occasionally one is requested
to stop a train in its tracks,
pull a child from a river,
or lie down with a hiker
lost days in the snow—
the angel equivalent
of a triple A call.
It's the rare angel who's
asked to stop a war.

Nevertheless, the angel returns
insufferable with accomplishment,
and proclaims over bingo,
"You should have been there, seen
the way I put my shoulder to the train."
Angels understand
the nick of time.
Though cautioned against it
a thousand thousand times—
angels are filled to bursting
of their diaphanous beings
with pride.
Overweening,
over arching everlasting pride.

Traveler in Paradise

The guidebook says: *air redolent of herbs.*
On the road from Arles to Aix,
Van Gogh to Cezanne,
they travel amid a cloud of fragrant happiness.

At the patisserie in Aix
the baker packs their lunch in bags
white and crisp as his jacket.
The morning light is golden oil,
a sentimental vision,
but she thinks *halo, anoint,*
as light pours over the baker's wife
arranging croissants on a tray.
When he learns they're from Los Angeles,
the baker says, "Ah, Paradise."

Ah, paradise! Violence and smog.
Real estate and cell phones.
They lunch on baguettes and wine
in the shadow of Mont Sainte-Victoire
looking down at ochre roofs
among the blue-green poplars.
Their favorite travel story:
imagine not recognizing paradise.

He wants a swimming pool:
 twenty by forty, perfect rectangle.

Sundays in the car,
real estate section of the *Times*
in her lap, traveling from suburb
to suburb until they find new houses
going up, lots big enough to dig
the pool lengthwise, leaving room
for a long green lawn for the boys to play on.

Pool finished, filled,
they float on their backs in antiseptic water.
He says, we need a dog.

She longs for a garden,
digs up the lawn to plant lavender, sage, fennel.
Rosemary only grows
in the gardens of the righteous,
but she plants it anyway.
Bougainvillea on the back fence,
morning glory on the side,
native plants for luring butterflies,
cupped red flowers
hummingbirds will drink from.
The summer garden: basil, tomatoes.

The neighbor to the rear dreams
of turrets and finials.
He tears down his old house
and chainsaws snags
where sparrow hawks nest.
With an army of workers,
he builds a stucco palace.

From the kitchen, she watches a hummingbird
shimmer red, green, blue as it flies
into the window,
its neck a snapping twig against the glass.
In death, color drains.
The glitterer becomes another dun-colored bird
falling to the ground.

She tells the story over dinner:
tomatoes layered with basil, fresh mozzarella,
all dappled with oil, vinegar—
the *caprese* they loved so in Florence.

He answers an ad in the *Times* under Poodle Rescue,
comes home with a black standard pup.
Their little boy, playing around the corner,
runs home when he sees a dog
in the car with his dad.
She's in the front yard with the other boys,
watches them approach, spill onto the lawn—
arms, legs, laughter, licking.

It's the lucid moment in dream:
the denouement of the mystery
with everyone gathered in the parlor.
She closes her eyes against seeing,
so painful is the light.

Traveler, Return

Slowly, the landscape
of my dream is changing—
the sandy berm, the ocean
to the end of sight—
unlike the old garden, bright
trellis of bougainvillea,
us safe in thorny profusion.

* * *

I dream that falling asleep
on your side of the bed
will lead me to you in the night.
I leave a map unfolded on the table.
Will you mark my route?

* * *

Last night you arrive
at the terminus of dream
wearing a miner's hat,
flannel shirt, and jeans,
covered with dirt,
smelling sweetly of sweat.
I struggle to hold you,
but you pull free
saying you want to shower,
have traveled so far,
have so much to wash clean.

Traveler

You come at night to say you're leaving,
have dreamed of freedom for so long.
And more, you love another—old familiar song.
I call for Mother in my grieving,
but in her own dream, she's not speaking.
The children, uninvolved, won't say you're wrong.
Our friends are not surprised, say don't prolong
the misery, the pain, by not accepting
that you're gone. Because I refuse to hear
the first time you say you really have to go,
you speak again, louder than before, and wear
a new love on your arm, gesture meant to show
you have no love for me—I must forbear.
The dead are even colder than we know.

From *The Green Season*

The birds they sang
at the break of day
Start again
I heard them say . . .

—Leonard Cohen

Gesture

My hand is raised,
as if to wave,
when I emerge from the sea,
mask and snorkel askew.
My friend who snaps this picture
thinks I'm greeting him.
But, no.
I'm holding my sliced palm
above my heart,
primitive gesture meant
to stay the flow of blood.
I've been tossed to coral
again
in the midst of bliss.

Madeleine

I think of you lying on the couch,
days after the birth of our boy—
your grandson—how your sobs
awakened me from fitful sleep
that first morning home.
You'd come to care for me, the baby,
your bewildered son.
Between the tears you said that no one loved you,
and now, surrounded by all this life,
you felt still more alone.
I watched you cry
as if watching a foreign movie,
in a language I couldn't speak.
I searched for meaning in what I saw:
your hair the color of bourbon
in the almost empty bottle
beside you on the floor.
I watched your face, still beautiful
un-mottled, smooth.
But I listened un-moved,
while you complained that I failed
to appreciate all you'd done—
marigolds planted by the back door,
the freshly laundered sheets.
Later, fueled by still more bourbon,
you started a fire
drying socks on the old gas stove.

I told your son to send you home
or I would take the baby and go.
Deep in my fertile life
I couldn't fathom such unhappiness,
didn't know the other meaning of passion,
had no language for such hunger,
had no language for such grief.

Domestic Arts

I am a young mother
so bored staying home
I agree to play Bridge
with my neighbors,
whom I suspect put up with me
to find a fourth to fill the table.

They are goddesses of domestic arts,
and between games hold forth
on finer points of decoupage, macramé
and the transformation of cans
into casseroles.

Still I am smug,
for I have gifts of my own:
precognitive dreams
and *gift of the phone*,
which I demonstrate by chanting
Mother Mother Mother Dear
call me now while my friends are here,
and when the phone rings
they are believers.

Because I love an audience,
I tell them my dreams:
how I see trash cans burning
the night before they burst in flame
behind my house,
how Papa's heart attack
awakens me from sleep.
How I knew the night before she labored
Jan's baby boy would be born dead.

Now the neighbors play three-handed games—
Pinochle, Euchre—
keep their children indoors,
cross against the light
when they see me coming.

Joined

Our kitchen, winter Sunday
boys playing on the floor,
I'm drying breakfast dishes
when I have the vision:
four chairs in front of a store
on a street I never travel.
Four chairs that will complete
our chair-less dining room suite.
I drive into the vision
and they are there,
with the same turned legs,
the same dark wood
as our furniture at home.
And on the bottom of one seat:
1927, date in the same hand
as on the table, underneath.

Everything sundered
wants reuniting,
everything rent, to mend.
So, I am not amazed Dear Heart
that nightly you walk
from the occluded country
to rest awhile with me.
Are not we
who have born three sons,
more joined than chair and table
turned from a single tree?

The Boy in the Bay

The boy in the bay is wailing again,
chest deep in water
from the first hour of summer
until the light fails,
the boy in the bay wails.
In winter, he cries
behind walls
muffled by stucco
 and wood,
but in summer in the gleam
of sunlight on water
as sailboats and kayaks glide by,
the boy in the bay wails.
Is this keening
a service he renders
because we're
embarrassed to cry
amid pleasure boats,
sandcastles, bright
striped umbrellas,
because it would seem
ungrateful to grieve
under the soft summer sky?

He Who Takes my Sorrow Away

He who takes my sorrow away
my friend has named her lover.
Who wouldn't wish for this,
if only for an hour or two,
that sorrow might
be lifted with the skirt,
discarded like a soiled shirt.

Red Roses

Because my kitchen overlooks
the boardwalk where we once walked
I see you turn, face my balcony,
and for a moment look into the house.
I am scrambling late breakfast eggs.
My dog, who once loved you, goes on eating
her kibble, doesn't announce
your presence with her customary bark.
I stir the eggs and quell the urge
to call out for you.
Can you see from your vantage
the twelve red roses in the tall vase?
The buds are tight and full of promise.
I was up late last night, got up late
this morning, but still in time
to glimpse your face as you walk
past my house, past my open window.

Waste

To change the water, I pluck
last week's tulips from their vase,
but the turbans unhinge in my hands,
orange cups upend in the sink,
with underside bands
of stem-colored green revealed.
A still life subject, I think:
tulips in their disrepair.

My love is a painter. Daily I tell him,
paintings are everywhere
but poems, my dear, are rare.
I am not a painter,
so I drop the old petals into a sack
with over-ripe cheese, uneaten fruit
and down the back stairs I march
the whole tableau to the trash.

The Green Season

O sweet morning—
coffee on the patio,
the Sunday *Times*
spread between us,
red geraniums
in the window box,
the dog at your feet.
Stop, Love. Don't move.
Don't even breathe.
I wish us fixed
this way, cups raised
the green season before us.

What God Wants

God has given you this beautiful day, and what have you given God?
—Man in front of Union Station, Los Angeles

I can't imagine God
wants a fatted calf. Surely, She knows better
than to feed on a fad
diet. As for sacrificing
firstborns, that's been
done to death.
Perhaps God would like
something in cashmere.
How about a Rolex?
Or bright yellow Hummer
that says *get out of my way!*
Maybe God is not
a glutton for consumption,
but an over-worked
mother who wants a day off
to lie on the sofa,
sip Diet Coke and watch Oprah—
a little peace
and quiet for once.
Someone else to pick up the kids
and make dinner
while She soaks in the tub.

Then later, with everyone seated
around the same table,
She would like just one meal
where no one spills milk
or complains
about the food set before him,
no one kicks at her brother
or pinches his sister.
Just one meal
to be eaten in gratitude
to be eaten in peace,
is that too much to ask?
Is that too much to want?

Credo

I believe in the Tuesdays
and Wednesdays of life,
the tuna sandwich lunches
and TV after dinner.
I believe in coffee with hot milk
and peanut butter toast,
Rosé wine in summer
and Burgundy in winter.

I am not in love with holidays,
birthdays—nothing special—
and weekends are just days
numbered six and seven,
though my love
dozing over TV golf
while I work the Sunday puzzle
might be all I need of life
and all I ask of heaven.

From *The Congress of Luminous Bodies*

Row, row, row, your boat
gently down the stream
merrily
merrily
merrily
life is but a dream.

Naked in an Open Boat

"A man that is born falls into a dream like a man who falls into the sea."
—Joseph Conrad

The boat is white
it has no sail
the sea is dark
my skin is pale
the night is hot,
but in the boat
if it were open
if I were bare
if the moon were new
I'd find you there

Where it Happened

At the seam of water and sand
a lone blue heron stands.
And in the placid sea
its distant kin: the pelican.
On such mornings
all birds are silver, all words are song:
silver water, silver light
birds in flight
and after.

Weeks ago, sirens
lured me from my work
and on my perch
above the beach, I watched
as lifeguards pulled
a girl from water to sand.
There is no way to sing this.

It is noon,
the light is not silver,
nothing is placid
the spectral birds elsewhere,
but two policemen are here
with a man and woman: the parents.
This is where it happened.

I didn't see her face
that day, only her torso
her pale arms, still legs.
And her swimsuit,
her scarlet swimsuit.

In the First Years

I don't know exactly what he does all day,
my fresh-pressed engineer
how his slide-rule calculates
movement buried in the passageways
of pipes and tanks.
He uses words like
volatile, effluent, pressure.

But, I know what I do
rumpled mommy of two,
in a neighborhood so strange
I think it dangerous to stroll them to the park
alone. Mostly, I stay home
and wash piles of laundry
I never sort or fold,
cook food that doesn't taste quite right,
although I won't admit
nothing's ever really good.

Sometimes I drive him to work
when I want the car to visit
my mother in the valley.
The refinery air is sulfurous
and thick, it makes the babies
in the back-seat gag, get sick,
vomit with such force they splatter my back
with flecks of puke, so I never
come entirely clean.

We go back after dusk
 to pick him up.
The air still stinks, but the tanks
light up like Christmas.
In a couple of years, the plant explodes
leaving a co-worker dead.
And, I will throw a plate of spaghetti
a whisper from my husband's head.
But in the first years, no notion
of what comes after—
the fragile welds that held us
a match strike from disaster.

Cover

The kitchen ceiling
in the rented house
is painted red.
At night, hopped up
on diet pills, I try
to paint it white.
Both sets of parents
offer money
for new clothes
if I drop
the baby weight.
So, I stay up late
wear a maternity smock
to cover my gown,
roll coat after coat
of cheap white paint
over the bleeding red.
Husband, babies, lie
sleeping in their beds.
Everything in *my* night
is florid, bright,
the whole world
back-of-the-eyelid red.

The Hen is More Tender Than the Tom

Thanksgiving, first holiday
away from the kitchens
of our mothers, our baby almost ready
in the pot beneath my skin,
I fix a turkey for our meal.
The bird and I are shaped the same:
all breast and belly atop
a pair of legs too thin
to hold such heft.

I put my hand into the opening
under her breast
and pull the sack of innards out.
Rub the cavity with salt
remembered words instruct.
Smear butter across her chest
Cover with a tin foil tent
Roast in a slow oven
until the flesh gives way.

I peel and mash potatoes,
mix green beans
and Campbell's soup, push
a cylinder of slithery red
from a can of Ocean Spray,
empty olives into a dish.
Don't forget to baste.
Make gravy, white and thick.

Husband takes the first hack
from the spot where the wattle had been,
finds a strange wand (was that once a neck?)
still lurking under the skin.

The Last Time I Fried a Chicken

The last time I fried a chicken,
baked home-made biscuits
with rolled-out dough
dusted with flour, cut
in circles with a jelly jar glass
The last time I fried a chicken
baked home-made biscuits
made creamy white gravy
from flour browned in grease
from Crisco fried chicken
milk added slowly
the other hand stirring
so no lumps form
The last time I fried a chicken
soaking pieces in a buttermilk
bath, dredging in flour
salt and pepper in a grocery
store bag, shaking each breast,
leg and thigh, then letting
them rest while Crisco
melts to sizzle in the cast iron
skillet, a gift from my Mimi
The last time I fried a chicken
baked home-made biscuits
made creamy pan gravy
His father came to dinner
woke up our babies
got them screaming and crying
asked, "What's your problem?"
My own face hotter than Crisco
the last time I fried a chicken.

Beans

Because his mother always
burns the beans
I am careful not to; but once
distracted by the babies at my feet
I let the pot run dry.
Slender fingers of green
ruin to brown with a minute's
inattention, but I refuse defeat
scrape the beans onto his plate
next to meatloaf and mashed potatoes.
He rolls his eyes
and I gather steam, become
the door-to-door salesman of supper:
They are *supposed* to look that way!
Burn-aise sauce, it's *French*, I say.
I saw the recipe on TV, or read it in a book.
Lies tumble from my lips like crumbs
and I invoke the saints of good cuisine:
Julia Child, Betty Crocker, Sara Lee,
so burned to a crisp am I by the thought
of doing wrong and getting caught.

Animal Zen

Tula the poodle
doesn't move or make a sound.
So still, she seems a piece
of garden kitsch.
And from the neighbor's porch
a statuary cat stares back.
They are content, it seems,
to serve one another
I and *thou*
subject and object
of meditation.
This is *the now*.
This is the suspension of time.
And, I can't help but wish
for a focus so intent, intense
for a symbiosis so benign.

Level

Spirit level it's called
this rectangular frame, vial
of liquid centered in the middle.
spirit center level
Not a yoga prop
but a mason's tool
like the one my father used
Saturdays, Sundays, weekdays
after work laying brick
around our house in the valley
mastering geometry
turning oblong to curve.
Curve around orange tree
after tree, laden
with blossom then fruit.
My father lay brick
on brick with a cunning sure hand.
And I imagine his pleasure
as he checked this work
and found it true,
the one thing he could do
to make his world level
to make his world right,
one brick after brick at a time.

We Planted

The plumeria we planted
by the front door
is blooming now
velvet yellow among
green leaves.
We didn't know the color
to expect then, when we placed
the root into the soil.
How hopeful is the act of planting!
But, how little we know of what takes hold
of what will flower
but not flourish
before the quick fall
to the ground.

Neophyte and the Swan

He shattered her glass
climbing over the table
to kiss her, that hot afternoon,
when she quoted his poem over wine.
It was free verse, abstract in part
and difficult, he knew
committing it to heart.
They kissed the afternoon away
and on the drive back, kissed
through every stop sign and red light.
Between the kisses
he smoked a cigarette.
And, what she failed to reconcile
about that day, was the casual way
he tossed the ember from the window
considering how hot and dry the summer
how much fuel there was to burn.

Bodies

Jupiter, Venus, the crescent moon
light up the night sky
and on the path below
we walk into our future
new as the moon, bright
as the planets aligned.
Always, the world awash in miracle!
And tonight, as if designed
for us, this congress
of luminous bodies.

Assembling the Soup

Finger the plug of stem
from tomato's plush belly,
crush the flesh between your palms.
O what satisfaction in the swish
and plop of pulp splashing
into the pot, in the thwack
of knife on wood mincing garlic,
dicing onion. All forms in flux
here, even the tiny beans
waiting in the glass bowl
are turning the water purple.

Perspective

From a sidewalk bench
 I watch N shrink
then vanish down
 Ben Yehuda Street,
looking for the pharmacy
he remembers.
We've walked so far in heat
my feet won't face another step.

The first half-hour or two
I'm happy for the rest.
But, when the sun declines
and the third man
comes on to me in Hebrew
then in English, I realize
I'm taken for a hooker
and my heart begins to race.

I grow certain that N
is maimed or dead.
Why else would he leave me here so long?
Jet-lagged and dazed, I'm sure
he's crossed against the red
and into traffic.

How long to wait before I flag police?

To feel light and free,
I'd left my stuff behind:
passport, camera, phone;
no shekels in my pocket,
just a key to the apartment
on a street whose name I can't recall
or if remembered
could not pronounce or find.

He comes back whole,
waving his arms in explanation.

I'm not angry or impressed,
lost now in my own story:
orphan girl, crumbs in her pocket,
living by wit alone in a strange
engrossing land.

Deshacer

I open the garage door
and our dog bounds free
across the street
disappearing down the alley,
her black form unmade
by the moonless night.
I panic, run in circles with the leash
but you calmly cross the street
calling her name.
Because she loves you
she lets you bring her home.

I won't repeat the dream
in which you leave me.
Let's just say I know the world,
how it alters in an instant,
that I awaken sick
in remorse and dread.
I can't face again the dinners
with other lonely women,
then late-night TV
until the dog and I can bear
to go to bed.

I don't need again to learn
the bitter lesson
that everything I love
is a flame between two fingers.

The Angel Garmin

Long have I wished for a calm voice
pointing me home
a confident voice telling which fork
in the forest road
leads to the soup, the bread
the welcoming bed
and which to dead-end
doom instead.

One night I circled a flat Texas town
for hours in my rented Ford
searching for the Hampton Inn
I'd left in daylight before
the unpredicted storm blew down.
The water rose; the gas gauge fell.
I surely had fore-tasted hell
lost in the unfamiliar, flooded town.

Now, the Angel Garmin takes
me through the four-level interchange
over cloverleaf and roundabout
keep left, exit, turn right
she tells me. Perfect
mother, guardian, guide
all knowing, but flexible, kind,
never scolding when I fail
to turn as I am told,
she simply *recalculates*
finds me, brings me back home.

Days Waiting

Days waiting
for the OB/GYN
days in line at the DMV
days stalled on the four-level-interchange
or queued at security LAX, JFK:
I want them back.
Days waiting for the rinse cycle
days waiting for the oven to heat
days waiting for water to boil
toast to pop up, butter to melt:
I want them back.
Days passed in cold hallways
days spent at bedside
days stuck in small chairs
waiting for bells, fearing alarms
days waiting for summer to start
days waiting for summer to end
days of migraine, nights of malaise
days of tedium, nights of dread:
I want them back
not for exchange, but to exclaim
this, too, my human life!

What to Believe: New Poems

Sunt lacramae rerum
There are tears for things

—Virgil, *Aeneid*

Nightingales are sobbing in the orchards of our mothers
from "Song of the Master and Boatswain"

—W.H. Auden,

Objects Brought From my Mother's House

*The aspects of things that are most important for us are hidden
because of their simplicity and familiarity.*

—Ludwig Wittgenstein

Ashtray

It looks like a skillet for elves,
this cast-iron ashtray
that once sat next to Father's
big chair and now sits
on the counter next to my stove.
A stirring spoon rests there.
But one time, as a child,
I left a smoldering pile of stubs
in its cradle. Caught,
I concocted a complex alibi
not yet having learned
the elegant recipe—like
making the crust of a pie,
few ingredients
and don't overwork it—
for a tasty, succulent, lie.

Green Pot

Chamber pot, spittoon
thunder mug—
rude music
in its names and uses—
this forest-green pot
my mother brought
from her grandmother's
farm after a century
of continuous service
to put in her own kitchen
where it held
generations of violets.
From this rough past
as catcher of human effluvia
and basin for blossoms
to my office
where it shelters
bouquets of pencils,
it has earned just one
tiny chip at its mouth.

Clay Figure

It looks sad,
the clay Madonna
I made in fourth grade
to be a gift
for Mother's Day.
Carefully painted,
but left unglazed
because Mrs. Gray
refused to fire it
with the good
children's work.
I had nothing else
to offer, so I gave
it to Mom anyway.
For the rest of her life
the unfinished figure
sat on her bookshelf,
wan, like a woman
too busy for make-up.
Now, amidst family
photos, knick-knacks,
and books, it sits
on my shelf, homage
to all who are plain,
broken, or marred,
but loved nonetheless
for their scars.

Mother's Gloves

I bring home the drawer
full of gloves: leather suppled
from a life of cold mornings,
damp nights.
Even hands in mild climates
grow cold, crave comfort,
close holding, want love.

I put on her gloves.

Purse: A Summation at Death

3 kinds of gum
5 wadded tissues
1 un-opened pack of tissues 1 set of keys
1 pair of bifocals
1 pair of sunglasses
1 wallet containing:
    1 credit card
    1 AAA card
    1 driver's license
    5 insurance cards
    20 dollars
1 compact
2 lipsticks
1 thumb-sized white plastic tube with a screw-off lid
5 foam earplugs
1 throat lozenge
1 penny

When I Open the Door

It scorches my face
like a slap: sweet odor
of Mother, trapped
in bags of jackets and hats,
in boxes of knick-knacks
and books, which sat
two days closed up in my car.

It sears my face
while I empty the car
with each parcel I mail
with each offering of books
each bag that I leave
for Goodwill: this perfume
of my mother disappearing.

Philosophy

If you are having trouble with this dream,
please contact our dream technician.

—The Dream Voice

Lingo

In college, I learned new words—
reification, nascent, inchoate—
hard to pronounce, even harder
to slide into conversation.
Ambiguity I loved, word describing
the world to me on my sail out
from the certain harbor of youth.
But *ambivalence* I made my own—
moving simultaneously toward
and away from what I loved,
fortress of the known unknown.

Supper: 3 Cans

Vienna Sausage
Pull ring tab
lay circle aside.
With thumb
and forefinger
dislodge sausage
bite, chew, swallow.
Note how jelly
aids the slide.

Deviled Ham
Unfold wrapper
with tempting
devils. Scrape
blisters of fat
from top. Discard.
Finger contents
onto saltine.
Think orphans.
Eat.

Spam
Suspiciously twist
key around can.
Careful!
One slip could slit wrist.
The oblong will stick
to side of can.
Use knife to spoil
suction. Bite
off hunk, pass
to neighbor.
Bail.

Philosophy

The British Prime Minister
fucks a pig in the first episode
of "The Black Mirror"
on prime-time TV, just as the terrorists
demanded, to save the princess
whom they'd kidnapped
before the first frame.
As incentive, they've presented
her severed finger in a box to prove
they're serious. Mean business.

Sorry to spoil it for you.

But, alas, all plots are spoiled
in this life slipping fast past satire
into theater beyond absurd.
What role would suit *you* to perform?
Terrorist? Princess? PM? Pig?
Me, I choose to play non-contemplating pig,
happy and innocent in my muck
until evil overtakes me from behind.

Tent

Malacosoma americanium

Not
a headless dancer
in diaphanous gown
mid-pirouette
above the ground,
but
a gauzy dress for
villains now at rest,
who, if loosed, could gnaw
the greeny forest down.

Lethologica

What's-his-name from My Dinner with Andre,
(not Andre) but Candace Bergen's sorry
Sex and the City blind date.

That old granny-shrub with small
petaled-blooms (pink or blue)
grown over-sized and round like a cabbage.

At various times, all three of Lear's
daughters caught (like kale between
incisor and canine) on their way out my mouth.

That parasol rising and falling
(as if water were wind) distant cousin
to the little ones, whose school

I disrupted, while swimming
(thinking, rubber bands from a shipwreck?)
to the reef miles from land,

tiny creatures that stung 300 welts
to one breast (before I lost count)
seven months after your death.

One Night, Three Dreams

An elf has picked me to go first
at a poetry lecture series.
My handouts are complete, but there
are not enough to go around. Though
my glasses slip from the perch of my nose
and I have not rehearsed, I plod on.
No one thinks my jokes are funny
or my examples apt.

It is Falcon Day. Falcons fill the sky,
and people fill the fields below. Everyone
runs in the direction of bird flight,
looking Elizabethan, like a movie
Midsummer Night's Dream.
O happy, happy, day,
orange balloons on long strings!

I serve communion from a loaf of bread
a little dish of butter on the side.
The celebrants want me to butter
the bread before placing it on their tongues.
I say, "For God's sake, this is the body
of Christ, not brunch!"

What to Believe

Nothing thicker than a knife's blade
separates happiness from melancholy.

—Virginia Woolf

Rambler

Brown, the color of dirt
and stick-shift to boot,
but cheap, as new cars go.
First "married" car bought
when our high school
love-mobile chugged to a halt.
"It's transportation," said
the husband. I wanted
nothing more than
to be transported,
didn't want to ramble,
wanted to fly.
On the first solo drive
I couldn't find reverse.
First Second Third
Onward
not counting the turns
it took to get there.

Use

There are days when even dirty
dishes make me happy: orange
plate, blue enameled pot, tiny net
for straining lemon seeds
from juice that tarts the soup.
I love the dishevelment
of the dish towel (orange too)
half in and half out of the sink—
stainless steel sink, still gleaming
under constant drops of water.

On the Drive Home from the
Jolly Party a Young Mother Confesses

Wrecked my life, she says,
of the South Dakota
Christmas, the two of them stuck
in a blizzard, alone in the truck.
No Sex-Education—you can guess
what happened. She turns
to the backseat, face
aflame in her story, *Wrecked,*
she repeats, and *Ruined.*

I want to offer solace,
but can't dislodge a word.
My husband, next to me,
mute as a mummy.
Her husband, at the wheel,
drives soberly onward.

I'm a young mother too,
just breaching my teens,
with a tale or two I could bare.
But, her candor scares me,
a game of Truth or Dare.
I sink deep into my seat,
pull my sweater up to my chin.
Quiet settles over us
cold and stifling ass now.

Dream Job

I want to pick up a mic and say what I think
I tell the counselor at Unemployment
When she asks, *What's your dream job?*
(me, nineteen, needing work between babies)
Honey, nobody cares what you think
(she, middle-aged, straddling kindness and candor)
In high school, I excelled in Speech and Debate,
didn't know my *dream job* answer was stupid
until the words spill from my mouth
and change the look on her face.
I'd been an actress too, could cry on demand,
Go to college, learn something, have something to say
but holding tears back was a script I'd not mastered.
She slides a box of tissue across the desk,
then a slip of paper with the address
of a spot needing a girl to mind the phone.
I give my nose a resounding blow.
Honey, when the phone rings, pick up, say hello.

Mrs. Pulver, Landlady

Let your knees be neighbors.
Mrs. Pulver's mother never
taught her that, so, when she came
to get the rent, I couldn't help
but see her panties
and the tops of her pull-up hose.
She liked to have a cup of tea
and tell me what I'd need
to know, now that I was grown,
about to have a baby of my own.
She'd repeat the story
of her terrible wreck,
gas-pedal stuck,
the zoom down the hill,
legs broken, pelvis crushed.
"If it happens to you, girl,
what will you do?"
Mrs. Pulver, whose pelvis
was pulverized
became a song in my brain:
duck and cover
kill the engine
don't lose the baby
down the drain.

Young Marrieds

We saved to buy new stuff when we had none
of the modern things, we thought would show
adults keeping house, not making soup from stone.
We bought a toolbox full of wrenches, a slow
cooker to braise cheap meat to taste.
We plunked nickels into coffee cans; expenses
we tallied carefully in a ledger, our faces
pinched, our fingers steady, for excellence
calls for sour concentration. How sweet
exceeding parents' expectations! We'd lie
before we'd ask their help with bills. We'd meet
our duty like a test of do or die,
and prove our right decision through our deeds—
stir the pot, fix the car, grimly pull some weeds.

Sweep Steak

The side of a dinner plate
will do, if you have no
tenderizer, tool
like a hammer with knuckles.
Lay the cheap steak on a wooden
slab and pound, pound, pound.
Don't speculate around the
whereabouts of old appetites
or you will overdo this step.
Unfurl a shroud of tin foil.
Heavy duty is best or you'll
need several sheets. Open
the envelope of soup
with your teeth. You might
feel a pang if tooth hits
aluminum. Never mind.
This pain has a short arc.
Sprinkle the meat with powder
and flake. Seal in foil. Crimp
edges. Place on a cookie sheet,
bake in a slow, slow oven,
until the pack howls at the door.

What to Believe

You worshipped at the *church of the open court*
in shorts, T-shirt, and red bandana
playing tennis, Sunday mornings, once
we'd given up on mass. Slow coffee and music
were a kind of church for me, so the boys and I stayed back
in our pajamas, tuned the radio to

94.7 a little bit of heaven KMET KMET

A bit of heaven too, the mere act of flipping
pancakes onto a stack, crowning with butter
and genuine maple syrup, pouring icy
milk into *Loony Tunes* glasses, giveaways
from the fast-food joint where we ate most Friday nights.

Breakfast with the Beatles, all the Beatles still alive,
darling children playing with their food,
our beloved dog licking syrup from the floor—
who could wish for more?

I did love Sunday mornings, but needed more than love.
I lacked the knack for easy pleasure.
Those days I didn't know what to believe,
so baffled was I by fury at the sight of you
walking freely in and out the door, whistling, happy,
your red bandana dripping sweat into my eyes
as you tried again and again to kiss me.

Nature

When carpet was plush or shag,
appliances Avocado,
or Harvest Gold, we bought
an eight-foot, down-back,
sofa from Ross Maher Home
in Garden Grove. Castle Coin
the color was called,
but really it was yellow
threaded with gold, echoing the tile
in the big coffee table
we'd found at Bullocks Lakewood.

Every suburb we shopped or lived
in was named to speak of nature:
La Palma, Cypress, Garden Grove
promised an arbor or shady glen.
But, our life was indoors
in the deep grass of green shag
under the light of swag lamps,
Our three babies climbing over
golden hills of sofa and chair.
The whirr of the vacuum, the blender,
the swish of dishes washing:
sweet enduring music of our sphere.

3rd Avenue North, Seattle

Look, Dear Heart, it's me
in winter cap and coat,
dressed, for once, for weather,
posed in front of the old apartment
where we were always cold
and often hungry. Meager haunt
of sauce-less spaghetti,
of peanut-butter and day-old bread.
You were a student here, studying
into the night while I read novels
and felt abandoned and unloved.
Sundays, I bawled on the phone
to Mother and you called your dad
to talk sports, laugh about my cooking.
Here is where I lay on the sofa
aflame with fever, where a punk
intruder punched your front teeth loose.
Here is where we fought every day,
made love every night.
Here is where we brought
our first two babies home.
Here is where we mapped
our sparkling future.
Here is where we couldn't wait to flee.
Now, the babies are grown
and you, Dear Heart, are gone.
But, you would recognize this place,
it's just as we left it—
the faded paint, the splintered door
opening to the asphalt lot.

Mother Sees an Angel at the Foot of her Bed

Tears are round, the sea is deep:
Roll them overboard and sleep
      from "Song of the Master and Boatswain"

                    —W.H. Auden

Dark Spring

I think it hard to hold onto belief
that spring's eternal glory will rebound
again, on days so dark and filled with grief
the sky hangs down. I hear the keening sound
of foghorns, far from shore where warning words
are useless, with no one to hear the soft
rejoinder to beware. Even seabirds
don't appear, find a distant home aloft.
Some happiness mistakes a cry for song.
So too, some misery's notes are crossed
with joy, and life and death belong
to the same mad throng. All that is lost
in winter, each spring returns to claim.
That I might fail to notice is my shame.

Avocado

Avocado, she wanted,
giving way at the end,
end yet un-dreamt
at the bend of mid-winter.
Avocado, she wanted
that odd creamy fruit,
fruit unheard of by girls
from rhubarb and peaches
in small-town Oklahoma.

That far-away summer
when she'd failed to stop weeping
you'll stop weeping, said the doctor
from big-town Oklahoma
with a thousand miles between
you and your mama.

She drove west on 66
until its end at the ocean,
ocean where her new world unfurled
under trees bearing fruit,
fruit like a fist
or a mottled green womb.
One taste, *avocado,* was just
what she wanted. Good Lord,
she knew she was home.

Catching Her Dance

Mom looks straight at me
through too-big glasses,
hands a blur like birds in flight.
She's *Chattanooga Cho-Cho-ing*
throughout the house to get me
off her back, prove she can still move,
if *she* feels like moving.

I grew up watching her dance
across the slick linoleum
of our kitchen floor
to *In the Mood* and other tunes
from her teens and World War II.

I try to catch her dance
on video, but my phone is new
and I don't know much about
the camera. What I am left with
is this awkward still shot,
snapped the moment she orders
put down that cell phone, Junie,
and watch me dance!

Aunt Lucy and Mother Surprise Me with a Visit

I dash frantic room to room
spread a bed, pick up toys,
kick dog bones into corners.
Before I can change my rumpled shirt
or brush my hair,
the dervishes rush the door.
Mother straightens every painting
in her path. Aunt Lucy arranges
knick-knacks on the mantle.
Mother suggests I fold laundry
as I go. Lucy says to try
some *Mop and Glo.* They'd
love to put my house in order
if they just had time to loiter.
Outside, the dogs drag trash across
the lawn. Of course, they see this
through my smudgy kitchen window.
I plop a can of tuna in a bowl,
whack celery, onion, pickle
to a furious fine mince, finish
with a squirt of mustard,
glop of mayo, rip open a bag
of chips and call it *lunch.*
They eat. They split a Coke.
Then, out they whirl
as quickly as they came.
On the porch, kisses, quick good byes.
Then Mother runs her thumb
hard down my spine,
her wordless gesture says it all:
straighten up, young lady, it's past time.

Aunt Lucy on the Phone

She claimed a new vocabulary
with her language juggling stroke—
words like *wicket*
pop up in place
of names and curses.
New worries too: she asks
is the ocean okay?
when I say *yes,* she then insists
the face on TV
was sent to kill her daughter.
She's angry when I tell her
it's not so.
What hasn't changed
is her concern for family;
though I must remind her
who I am, she asks
over and over if I'm okay.
And before goodbye, the last words
I'll ever hear her say—
I'm so glad you have a living world today.

Forgiving Fish

Salmon is forgiving fish
I tell my brother.
Lean protein, good oil,
so many ways to cook—
poach, grill, bake, broil
and juicy enough to survive
a momentary inattention.
Even over-done, delicious.
And, when salmon's not
in season, you can eat
it from a can with mayo
and a squirt of lemon,
if you have a lemon on hand.
When we were kids,
Mother bound canned salmon
with eggs, saltines,
shaped the pink into rounds,
dusted with flour, then fried
in spitting Crisco.
Salmon patties, the only fish
she ever cooked,
because, she said, *fish stinks*
and *I don't know how to fix it.*

May 10, 1934, Berlin

". . . the gradual rise of Nazi Germany, which somehow took the laissez-faire, un-radicalized citizens of Berlin by surprise."

—Benjamin Lindsay, *Vanity Fair*

Aunts clad in dark dresses and pearls
and dapper uncles in fine worsted suits,
gather at the table laden for pleasure:
flowers, champagne, frosted cake,
and a crystal decanter of sherry.
Father is poised to offer a toast,
Mother, in profile, appears morose,
but the absent daughter smiles
from the photograph placed
at the center of plenty.
May 10, 1934, Berlin, beloved girl
gone off to Palestine, alone.
How will she celebrate her birthday?
Has she made friends?
Surely, she's lost her mind, leaving
such comfort, love, and family behind.

Mother Sees an Angel at the Foot of Her Bed

Before the spill of stars
the shatter, scatter
across the hemispheres
before the tremble, tremor
before the Grand quake
when *astrocyte* was a word
not a word made flesh,
she wakens to the stir
of wings rustling, settling
at the foot of her bed.

The angel sits with her
for seven nights.
His country-doctor gaze
is a beam of light, comforting
her as a father comforts
his dream-tossed child.
She is lonesome when he goes.
In his backward glance
her world ignites, explodes.

Mother Returns

Mother returns, as she might, from a cruise,
dressed not in black, but chartreuse.
Robust, tan, and tall, not pekid, not frail,
like when she packed in her life and set sail.
I'm warmed to accept her familiar embrace,
but startled to notice she's wearing my face.

Nabisco Original Saltine

Working class cousin
of a crouton, I am crushing
you between my palms into a bowl
of Campbell's Tomato Soup.
Sometimes I spread you with butter
or P & J, or make four tiny
sandwiches with a quartered slice
of American yellow cheese.
Cracker I once eschewed
for fancier crackers, I take you back.
You are trusty like old love,
the only cracker, when washed down
with Coke, able to soothe my queasy belly.
My grandpa broke a sleeve-full
into a bowl, topped the crumbles
with whole milk, sometimes
on summer nights, for supper.

Green Fire

My brother says he fears
the fire, since rain
has come and sun-burnt
hills seethe green
in shrub and flower.
I've heard the tales,
but never seen
the flash of green at sunset.
I strain for faith
in what remains unseen. If it's true that each
contains the seed of other,
then I too expect to see the fire burn green.

Once, Time

Once, time trickled slowly
like sap in winter,
a Russian novel's trudge
through snow. Time enough
to break the plate,
retrieve the pieces,
break the bone and set
it once again in place.
Now, I fear what cracks
will not be mended.
I walk carefully. Everywhere
the path is slick and fast.

Acknowledgements

I would like to thank the editors of the following publications in which some of the poems in the new section, "What to Believe," have appeared, sometimes in slightly different form or under another title:

Chiron Review: "Ashtray," "Catching Her Dance," "Dream Job," "Forgiving Fish," "Gloves," "Green Fire," "Green Pot," "Nature," "What to Believe"

Mas Tequila Review: "Aunt Lucy and Mother Surprise Me with a Visit," "When I Open the Door"

Nerve Cowboy: "3rd Avenue North, Seattle," "Once, Time Trickled Slowly," "Use"

New Verse News: "Philosophy"

Rattle: "Rambler"

RCC Muse: "Young Marrieds"

Rise Up Review: "Philosophy"

Silver Birch: "Clay Figure"

Verse-Virtual: "3rd Avenue North, Seattle," "On the Way Home from the Jolly Party, a Young Mother Confesses," "What to Believe," "When I Open the Door"

Further thanks to editors Michael Hathaway of *Chiron Review,* Marilyn Johnson and Joan Jobe Smith of *Pearl,* and David Caddy of *Tears in the Fence* whose magazines were the site of first publication for a preponderance of the poems in the "selected" sections of *Gravity: New and Selected Poems.*

A special thank you to Firestone Feinberg of *Verse-Virtual* who, on a monthly basis, has given a second home to many of the poems in all sections of the book.

Thanks to Jerod Santek for the generous residencies at *Write On Door County* in beautiful lakeside Wisconsin, which allowed time to complete this book.

Much gratitude to Mifanwy Kaiser for making this book a reality.

Finally, Love and gratitude to Jill Young, who has been first reader, final reader, editor, one woman workshop, and dearest friend since we met in a creative writing class at California State University, Long Beach, many years ago.

Also Available from Moon Tide Press

My Kidney Just Arrived (Second Edition), G. Murray Thomas (2025)
Reluctant Prophets, J.D. Isip (2025)
Enormous Blue Umbrella, Donna Hilbert (2025)
Sky Leaning Toward Winter, Terri Niccum (2024)
Living the Sundown: A Caregiving Memoir, G. Murray Thomas (2024)
Figure Study, Kathryn de Lancellotti (2024)
Suffer for This: Love, Sex, Marriage, & Rock 'N' Roll,
        Victor D. Infante (2024)
What Blooms in the Dark, Emily J. Mundy (2024)
Fable, Bryn Wickerd (2024)
Diamond Bars 2, David A. Romero (2024)
Safe Handling, Rebecca Evans (2024)
More Jerkumstances: New & Selected Poems, Barbara Eknoian (2024)
Dissection Day, Ally McGregor (2023)
He's a Color Until He's Not, Christian Hanz Lozada (2023)
The Language of Fractions, Nicelle Davis (2023)
Paradise Anonymous, Oriana Ivy (2023)
Now You Are a Missing Person, Susan Hayden (2023)
Maze Mouth, Brian Sonia-Wallace (2023)
Tangled by Blood, Rebecca Evans (2023)
Another Way of Loving Death, Jeremy Ra (2023)
Kissing the Wound, J.D. Isip (2023)
Feed It to the River, Terhi K. Cherry (2022)
*Beat Not Beat: An Anthology of California Poets Screwing
        on the Beat and Post-Beat Tradition* (2022)
*When There Are Nine: Poems Celebrating the Life and Achievements
        of Ruth Bader Ginsburg* (2022)
The Knife Thrower's Daughter, Terri Niccum (2022)
2 Revere Place, Aruni Wijesinghe (2022)
Here Go the Knives, Kelsey Bryan-Zwick (2022)
Trumpets in the Sky, Jerry Garcia (2022)
Threnody, Donna Hilbert (2022)
A Burning Lake of Paper Suns, Ellen Webre (2021)

Instructions for an Animal Body, Kelly Gray (2021)
Head *V* Heart: New & Selected Poems, Rob Sturma (2021)
*Sh!t Men Say to Me: A Poetry Anthology in Response
    to Toxic Masculinity* (2021)
Flower Grand First, Gustavo Hernandez (2021)
Everything is Radiant Between the Hates, Rich Ferguson (2020)
When the Pain Starts: Poetry as Sequential Art, Alan Passman (2020)
This Place Could Be Haunted If I Didn't Believe in Love,
    Lincoln McElwee (2020)
Impossible Thirst, Kathryn de Lancellotti (2020)
Lullabies for End Times, Jennifer Bradpiece (2020)
Crabgrass World, Robin Axworthy (2020)
Contortionist Tongue, Dania Ayah Alkhouli (2020)
The only thing that makes sense is to grow, Scott Ferry (2020)
Dead Letter Box, Terri Niccum (2019)
Tea and Subtitles: Selected Poems 1999-2019, Michael Miller (2019)
At the Table of the Unknown, Alexandra Umlas (2019)
The Book of Rabbits, Vince Trimboli (2019)
Everything I Write Is a Love Song to the World, David McIntire (2019)
Letters to the Leader, HanaLena Fennel (2019)
Darwin's Garden, Lee Rossi (2019)
Dark Ink: A Poetry Anthology Inspired by Horror (2018)
Drop and Dazzle, Peggy Dobreer (2018)
Junkie Wife, Alexis Rhone Fancher (2018)
The Moon, My Lover, My Mother, & the Dog, Daniel McGinn (2018)
Lullaby of Teeth: An Anthology of Southern California Poetry (2017)
Angels in Seven, Michael Miller (2016)
A Likely Story, Robbi Nester (2014)
Embers on the Stairs, Ruth Bavetta (2014)
The Green of Sunset, John Brantingham (2013)
The Savagery of Bone, Timothy Matthew Perez (2013)
The Silence of Doorways, Sharon Venezio (2013)
Cosmos: An Anthology of Southern California Poetry (2012)
Straws and Shadows, Irena Praitis (2012)
In the Lake of Your Bones, Peggy Dobreer (2012)
I Was Building Up to Something, Susan Davis (2011)

Hopeless Cases, Michael Kramer (2011)
One World, Gail Newman (2011)
What We Ache For, Eric Morago (2010)
Now and Then, Lee Mallory (2009)
Pop Art: An Anthology of Southern California Poetry (2009)
In the Heaven of Never Before, Carine Topal (2008)
A Wild Region, Kate Buckley (2008)
Carving in Bone: An Anthology of Orange County Poetry (2007)
Kindness from a Dark God, Ben Trigg (2007)
A Thin Strand of Lights, Ricki Mandeville (2006)
Sleepyhead Assassins, Mindy Nettifee (2006)
Tide Pools: An Anthology of Orange County Poetry (2006)
Lost American Nights: Lyrics & Poems, Michael Ubaldini (2006)

Patrons

Moon Tide Press would like to thank the following people for their support in helping publish the finest poetry from the Southern California region. To sign up as a patron, visit www.moontidepress.com or send an email to publisher@moontidepress.com.

Anonymous
Robin Axworthy
Conner Brenner
Nicole Connolly
Bill Cushing
Susan Davis
Kristen Baum DeBeasi
Peggy Dobreer
Kate Gale
Dennis Gowans
Alexis Rhone Fancher
HanaLena Fennel
Half Off Books & Brad T. Cox
Donna Hilbert
Jim & Vicky Hoggatt
Michael Kramer
Ron Koertge & Bianca Richards
Gary Jacobelly
Ray & Christi Lacoste

Jeffery Lewis
Zachary & Tammy Locklin
Lincoln McElwee
David McIntire
José Enrique Medina
Michael Miller &
Rachanee Srisavasdi
Michelle & Robert Miller
Ronny & Richard Morago
Terri Niccum
Andrew November
Jeremy Ra
Luke & Mia Salazar
Jennifer Smith
Roger Sponder
Andrew Turner
Rex Wilder
Mariano Zaro
Wes Bryan Zwick

www.ingramcontent.com/pod-product-compliance
Lightning Source LLC
Chambersburg PA
CBHW031138090426
42738CB00008B/1140